I CAN
LIVE

I CAN
LIVE

David T. Brand Jr.

XULON PRESS

2301 Lucien Way #415
Maitland, FL 32751
407.339.4217
www.xulonpress.com

Unless otherwise indicated, Scripture quotations taken from the King James Version (KJV) – *public domain*.

Printed in the United States of America.

Paperback ISBN-13: 978-1-6628-0538-7
eBook ISBN-13: 978-1-6628-0539-4

CONTENTS

PART I : WHAT DO I SAY TO MYSELF

Part II: What Has God Said To Me

To my little flock:

Shirley, my salt my sugar. My wife. Thank you for loving me, and knowing me almost as long as I've known myself. We have cleared many hurdles together and have a couple more to go. I made you a few promises and I plan to have them all crossed off before it's all said and done. Love you.

Solomon, the royal heir and my firstborn son. This is for you. Always believe in yourself. Sometimes other will, sometimes they won't, you are a man of wisdom. A man of intelligence. A man of strength. I love you more than you'll ever know.

Rachel, my beautiful, oldest daughter. This is for you. Always believe in yourself. I know you do! I've seen you grow with my own eyes. You were dancing for a crowd of one even before we could understand. Don't ever change my beautiful girl.

Leah, my beautiful, youngest daughter. You seem have been here before. Your soul is old, rich in compassion and genuine concern for people. I hope you never lose that. People need that. They may never say it, but they do, and when they do, I hope they meet you. Don't ever change my beautiful girl.

Asa, the youngest and last king of the family. I love your tenacity. I know you were able to develop this because you have two older lions watching over you in your big brother and your father. You've learned to not be afraid. I hope that remains with you all your life. You are a great man, Asa. I love you more than you'll ever know.

FOREWORD

> *"What you say can preserve life or destroy it; so you must accept the consequences of your words"*
> Proverbs 18:21, Good News Translation.

Have you ever wondered how the how the bible has retained its timeless appeal over the years? This collection of writings from various Middle Eastern ascetics, prophets, poets, and even fishermen and common laborers has lasted for millennia. This longevity speaks to the fact that the words contained therein are not just the humble words of flawed people, but something more. The power, purpose, and principles contained in these often-gilded pages cannot be denied. There are narratives within its pages that stretch the mind and even the heart. These factors assure that the bible's pages transcend simple stories to become sacred scriptures.

I believe that this inerrant collection of texts is the foundation for building a successful life. It is scriptures like the one above that frame and undergird the declarations and affirmations that you are about to read. What you say and how you think matters. From these factors flow who you are. These declarations are not an attempt at replacing for the word of God, but drawn from the deep well of its wisdom. This is a carefully curated collection designed to be a platform from which we can launch into the endless realms of better.

I have known the author of this book for some time. He is a dynamic and powerful teacher, preacher, and wise (and licensed) counselor. One of the most over-riding and profound things about David is his intense passion for the word of God. For David, the word is not just a part of life; it is life itself. Out of the heart flow the issues of life, therefore David has resolved to hide the word of God within his own heart.

It is with this utmost compassion that the author has penned this series of powerful declarations to share with you. Each affirmation is thoughtfully crafted and filled to bursting with the word of God, so that reader will find the word of God flowing out of his or her own mouth and heart. In these turbulent times, the word of God is more important than ever. The stability and power of these life-filled words have not lost their effi-cacy. Grass will wither, flowers will fade, and heaven and earth will pass away, but the word of God will remain forever. Prepare to embark on a journey to better with David Brand, and declare these life-changing words over yourself and your life!

~David Wallace

YES,
YOU
CAN

Introduction

Out of adversity was birthed strength. That is often the case in life. You can allow your situation to dictate and talk to you or you can move in faith and talk back. Most of us live with doubts. We are harder on ourselves than anyone outside of us could ever be...because we know our own capacities. We see our dreams, we can only describe to others. When things go terribly wrong it is why people don't always understand our responses, our internal pictures of the situations are different. Sometimes we try to explain but it is still not clear. This book was written from one of those places of perspective. This book was written while wrestling through the night like Jacob. It was through the entangled emotions that these affirmations were birthed. When I had no one to tag in, I tagged myself through the power of the Eternal Creator. I spoke over myself, through the tears, through the pain, through the frustration, through the embarrassment, until I recovered. This book was written to remind us of two voices out of all the others in the world that mean and produce the most; our own and the voice of God. It is my hope and prayer that you will hear your own while reading mine and be reminded of His as you read through this book.

"There Is Good in Me"

I am a man. **I am made in the image of the Eternal Creator**. *There is good, naturally in me.* I have strengths. I have things I do well. I can also create. I can lead. I can think well. I can show compassion. I can forgive. I can resist temptation. I can sacrifice for others. I can carry the load. I can manage my emotions. I can rebound after hard times. I can be vulnerable.

"It Didn't Break Me"

I am emotionally strong. I am a survivor. It happened. It was real. I am not broken. *It didn't break me.* I survived. I am well. I am stronger. I am wiser. I can learn from my experiences. My experiences teach me. I learn. My experiences build me. My experiences help me to fill my heart and memory with gratitude. I can cope with things I can't change. I can change certain things about my life. I am not stuck. I am not stagnant. I have the strength to move forward. I am not afraid. I am not confused. I am well. I am whole. I am the man, I am the woman God made me to be. I am a work in progress.

"Like a Tree, Planted by Rivers of Water"

I know how to go through the changes of life. I will keep my eyes on Christ. I know who I am. I know who I've been. I know who I'm not. I know my role. I have peace within. I will focus on what is important. I will focus on what feeds me. I will embrace challenges with courage and faith. **I am spiritually settled.** I will plant my feet. I will carry my cross. I will not waver. I will commit to growth. I will protect my growth. I will harness my capacity. *I will flourish like the tree, planted by rivers of water.*

"I Can Be Successful"

I can do it. I can succeed. **I am capable**. I am making progress. I am growing. I am moving forward. I am doing better. I am pressing forward. I am rising higher. I am determined. I believe there is more for me. I know there is more for me. I can handle more. I can manage more. *I can be successful in any environment*. I can provide for my family. I can build up other men. I can lead.

"My Mind Is My Greatest Weapon"

I am made in God's image. I have the mind of Christ. I can think. I can listen. I can understand. I am allowed to feel confused. I am not defined by confusion. I am not defined by mistakes. I can figure things out. I can learn new skills. I can teach what I know. I know what I know. There are things I do that can not be duplicated. *My mind is my greatest weapon*. My mind belongs to me. My thoughts belong to me. My dreams belong to me. I am in control of my thoughts. I will think well. I will feel well. I will think before speaking. I will think before acting. I will access more of who I am through thinking better. **I am intelligent**.

"I Am Ready for Depth"

I know how to love. I know when to love. I can be loved. I can adapt. I can change. I can sacrifice. I can care for the needs of others before mine. I can overcome how I used to be. I am better. My heart is healed. My mind is healed. I am ready to love. I am ready to move forward. *I am ready for depth*. I can go deeper. I am not afraid of love. I can learn how to love. **I am worthy of love**.

"I Am Not Afraid of Love"

I can learn to love better. I have love in my heart. I can be taught what love means. I can show my emotions. It's ok for me to show and share my emotions. I can share my thoughts. I can give of myself to another. I can trust. I can let my guard down. I can be vulnerable. *I am not afraid of love*. I can grow through relationships. I can heal through relationships. I know my limits. I am ok with boundaries. I understand boundaries. I can love when things are favorable. I can love when things are hard. **I am capable of loving**.

"Fear Will Not Force Me"

I **am not afraid**. I can meet obligations. I can be accountable to a variety of people and situations. Fear is not my boss. Fear does not define me. I am ok feeling afraid sometimes. I can manage my emotions when stressed. I know when to retreat. I know when to stand. I know when to be still. I know when to be silent. *Fear will not force me into another mistake.* I will take a deep breath. I will gather my thoughts. I will remember where my help comes from. I will be settled. I will be strong. I will be established. Fear is not my first, middle, or last name.

"Stretching Is Good for Muscles"

I don't understand all the time. I don't have the answers right now. I am not always sure. I don't know what is happening all of the time. I really don't want to do it. This is stretching me. I simply do not like this. This does not seem fair. Yet, I have peace. Yet I have comfort. Yet I feel strong. *Only because I've seen and heard over and over, stretching is good for muscles*. I've learned to be ok not being ok. **I am comfortable being uncomfortable.** Throw me in the furnace. I will not bow. Pour the drink, I'll drink the cup. Laugh at me, I'll laugh last. Send me, I'll go. I will stand alone in the garden, I will be ok. I was made for this.

"I WILL NOT DIE"

I know what it is like to be counted out. I have heard their words. I have seen their smirks. I still carry the scars. I will not surrender. I will not give in. I will not throw it all away. I will not crack. *I will not die*. I will not fail. I will not be stopped. **I will not quit**. I will not pass. I will not fold. I will not break. I will not miss. I will not strike out. I will not be disqualified. I will not listen to their voices. I will not compromise. I will not run. I will not walk away. I will not find an excuse. I will not create a distraction. I will not self-sabotage.

"I WILL SHOW UP WHEN CALLED UPON"

I **am brave**. I can face adversity. I can overcome weaknesses. I can pass tests. I can learn. I can admit when I need help. I can endure trials. I can stand still when I need to, knowing that God is fighting my battles. I will not run from my responsibilities. I will meet my obligations. I will rise to the occasion whenever presented with an opportunity. *I will show up when called upon*. I will keep my head lifted. I will sleep peacefully at night. I will rise with purpose in the morning. I will trust that God's plan is the best in my life.

Even though I am hunted in my own neighborhood. Even though my skin color comes with trauma. Even though no one seems to understand me. Even through the tears of frustration and pain, I am brave.

"I WILL FACE THE UGLY PARTS OF ME"

I am not ashamed. I understand my flaws. I know that sin can be an everyday struggle. I am getting better. I can recognize growth. I will not beat myself up. I will not project my pain onto others. *I will face the ugly parts of me*. I will acknowledge my sin before a forgiving God. I will acknowledge the pain I've caused to those who love me. I will forgive myself. I will hold my head up. I will not wallow in the past. I will apologize. I will reconcile. I will not focus on my failures. I will find new ways to cope when I feel down. I will learn to improve my outlets. I am not my mistakes. I can be a new creature through the redeeming love of Christ.

"THERE IS VICTORY IN MY LIFE"

I can win. I am victorious. I'm not defined by past experiences. I have learned from the past. I know how to win. I know how to lose. I know I can. I know how to be confident. Victory suits me. *There is victory in my life.* I have victory in my hands. I have victory in my heart. I have victory in my thoughts. I have victory in my emotions. I have victory in relationships. I have victory professionally. Winning feels good. I have more wins in me. I can show others how to win. I am not afraid of my own success. I deserve to win. I will experience the win. When I win, others benefit.

"I WILL LIVE THIS PURPOSE"

I have a purpose. I am unique. I am 1 of 1. There is not another person like me. People may look the same. People may talk the same. People may act the same, but no one is me. I am me. I am happy to be me. I love me. I was made to be me and no one else. I have a piece of God in my DNA, that means I am capable, I have value, and I was created with a purpose. I will find this purpose. *I will live this purpose*. I will find comfort in this purpose. I will embrace this purpose. I will not run from this purpose. I am excited about my purpose. My purpose is mine.

"I AM THE COLOR OF POWER"

I can break curses. I can chart new paths. I can be the first. I can blaze new trails. I can change my whole family history. I can do what they didn't do. I can do what they said I couldn't. I can do what they said I wouldn't. I can go farther. I can make more. I can see more. I can do more. I can be more. I am my ancestors' reason. I am prophecy fulfilled. I am a dream lived. I am the power of forward. I am the direction of change. I am the smell of victory. *I am the color of power*. I am the sound of thunder. I am the peace of rain. I am the comfort of the tide. I will not be held back. I will not make excuses. **I can overcome.** I will overcome.

God said we are made in His image. He breathed life into our nostrils. He sustains life. He grants us life. We have the divine in us.

Gen 1:26-29
Gen 2:7
John 10:10
I Cor 15:49
Col 1:16

> Resilience is a natural strength of every man, woman, and child born on the earth. We simply need an obstacle, faith and strength to produce the hidden power.

Job 1:21
Psa 34:19
Matt 16:24
II Cor 4:16-18
Phil 3:14

God promised moments of clarity and peace. Life will not constantly be like a shoe in the dryer. One day we will be content, be still, be settled.

Gen 2:1-3
Psa 138:8
Phil 1:6
Col 4:12
Jas 1:4

We are all born with incredible potential. That
potential can be unlocked and harnessed.
We can do incredible things when we
believe we can.

I Sam 30:6
Psa 100:3
Rom 8:37
Phil 4:13
I John 5:4

Our brains separate us from animals. We have incredible potential to harness our minds and use them in incredible ways. Our intelligence is a model in the earth.

Gen 2:19,20
Job 32:8
Job 35:11
Acts 22:3
Heb 11:6

We are worthy of love. We deserve love. Even when we are wrong. Even when we have failed. In the worst times of our life, we are still worthy of love. Love is supposed to be unconditional.

Deut 7:7
Ezra 9:13
Rom 5:8
Eph 2:4
I John 4:11

We have the capacity to love. If we can find
healing and peace, we can love. We have
the tools to love, we have to access them,
and use them.

Lev 19:18
Matt 22:39
Rom 5:5
Rom 12:10
II Pet 5:7

Fear is not the controlling emotion in my life.
It has it's place but I will not give it place
in my life. I will manage how I feel not my
circumstances. I can face anything. Fear is not
telling me the truth.

Num 13:30
Jos 14:12
I Sam 17:32
Psa 23:4
Isa 8:10

Life is not always fun. Life is not always easy. There are times I am in over my head. There are times when I am not sure. There are tasks that go against everything in me. I am finding comfort in the uncomfortable.

Ex 1:12
Psa 6:6
Psa 42:3
Dan 6:16
Luke 22:44

Resilience begins with our decisions. We must convince ourselves first of our goals. Once we are convinced our bodies as well as our minds are capable of astounding feats. We must not quit.

Ex 14:15
Isa 50:7
Lk 9:51
Matt 16:24
Rom 8:38

Champions begin in the heart and mind. We must have the faith to step out on ideas and even feelings. We can even use fear to our advantage and flip it into bravery.

Ex 14:15
I Sam 17:32
Psa 27:1
Psa 56:4
Heb 13:6

We no longer have to live in shame. God promised to take away the stain of sin from our life. He promised blessings and curses. Sin represents the curses that he took for us, leaving us free to enjoy the life of blessing.

Gen 3:10
Psa 51:3
Rom 5:5
Gal 3:13
Phil 3:13

When God blew breath into my nostrils, it was the wind of victory. All I do is win. My middle name is Victory. Winning suits me.

Gen 2:7
Job 42:10
Psa 98:1
I Cor 15:57
Phil 4:13

God took time to create the world. I was part of that creation and I also share in His purpose. I am one of his wonderful works.

Gen 2:7
Job 5:9
Psa 111:2
Psa 139:14
Eph 2:10

Overcoming is the result of faith, resilience, and strength. Even if defeated, overcoming is the result of a persistent fight. God promises victory to those who continue to fight.

Gen 22:13
Luke 23:34
Rom 8:31
Rom 12:21
Rev 21:7

CPSIA information can be obtained
at www.ICGtesting.com
Printed in the USA
LVHW081152190321
681671LV00040B/1723

9 781662 805387